JOHN WESLEY

by MAY McNEER *and* LYND WARD

Nashville　　ABINGDON PRESS　　*New York*

1170

ISBN 0-687-20429-1 (*Cloth*)
ISBN 0-687-20430-5 (*Paper*)

CONTENTS

A COTTAGE HOME

In England, in the county of Lincolnshire, three little rivers and a canal come together to make a small green island of the town of Epworth. This was the market town for a wild and rough farming country. Here the Reverend Samuel Wesley preached in a small church. Here his wife Susanna cared for their children in a cottage nearby. And here John Wesley was born on June 17, 1703.

A neighbor, brushing the path before her house, stopped to lean on her broom and talk to a passing woman. "They say there be another mouth to feed at the minister's house today."

The woman swung her empty market basket to the other arm and nodded until the ruffle of her cap flapped. "Aye, and another boy at last, after so many girls. The parsonage be nigh to bursting."

The cottage seemed to peer from its little windows anxiously at the world, as if wondering how long its old stone walls could stand the strain of this growing family. Its roof of thatched straw sagged lower and lower each season. Samuel, noticing that a small brown bird had built its nest in one corner, had fresh straw put on.

Samuel and Susanna gladly and proudly welcomed the new baby. John was the fifteenth child, and there were to be four younger ones. This home was a little world in itself. John could sniff the scent of musty straw from the roof all day as he staggered on his baby legs about the rough-hewn floors. His teeth chattered with the cold and damp of morning as he slipped out of bed. The kitchen was a big room, for such a small house. It was a good place, too, with its great chimney, the smell of warm bread, the sounds of pans and kettles, and of scouring and talk.

There were four tall grownups in the cottage. In the kitchen was a country girl. In the nursery was Nurse. And there were, of course, Father and Mother.

Young as he was, John realized that Mother was very strict. Even during the first three months of his life the baby Jack, as he was usually called, had been rocked to sleep in his cradle at certain times. And he had been taught to cry softly, when he must cry. Susanna Wesley kept a little switch handy to punish her children, but they did not often need to feel its sting. For when Father or Mother spoke to them, they obeyed. The cottage was always quiet and orderly. Mother had a place for everything, and everything must be kept where it belonged. She had each minute of each day arranged for some task. But she had a little time each day, too, for talk and for singing and sometimes for games and fun.

As small Jack bent his head and folded his hands, his father said grace with the earnestness of a man who tried to do good in the world. John sat close beside his mother, so that she might teach him proper manners as he ate. Susanna Wesley and her husband had both come from educated families. Mrs. Wesley had been a minister's daughter and one of twenty-five children. She and Samuel had no intention of letting their children grow up in the

6

rude and rough ways of this wild country.

There was never any finicky appetite at this table, except for illness. The Reverend Samuel Wesley had so little money that his wife was often at a loss to know where to get enough bread and meat and porridge for the day. She always looked kind, and always a little worried.

This was a hard time, one of those times when Father could not collect what was owed him from the farmers who were hired to grow his crops, and who were supposed to share the wheat or oats with the minister. From his chair beside his mother Jack could see his whole family. Next to Father was Samuel, long-legged and important in his place as the oldest child. He was making plans to go to London soon, to attend Westminster School for boys. Between him and Jack were the girls—Susanna, Martha, Mary, Emilia, and lively Hetty. All the Wesley girls were bright, and all of them were better educated than most girls. Yet, because they were so poor, they wore dresses patched and worn.

Now Mother was looking at Jack reprovingly. "Eat your bread and milk, Jack," she said.

But Jack clattered his pewter spoon against the bowl and drew back, shaking his head.

"I believe the child feels ill today," Mrs. Wesley said. "I shall put him to bed."

When he was in bed, Mrs. Wesley appeared with a bottle of medicine she had brewed from herbs. She placed the spoon against his lips and said, "Open your mouth, Jack. This is evil tasting, but 'twill do you good."

John's mouth popped open. His face puckered with the bitter taste, but he swallowed the medicine without a whimper. Before long he was back at his place at the long table, eating his porridge with the others.

During John's first two years several things happened to the family. His older brother Samuel went away to boarding school in London. Another baby replaced John as the youngest. This was a little girl called Anne. But, even as the household rejoiced in the new daughter, the minister grew more and more anxious. These rough, ignorant people from the farms about Epworth would not go to church. They did not even like to have a preacher in the village. They disliked it so much that they sometimes burned his crops or stole his cattle. Samuel Wesley had trouble with the farmers who were supposed to take care of raising his crops for him, for they would not work. His family had to be fed by his little farm, and he could not pay his debts.

Then, when John was two years old, there came a sad day. He hung back behind his sisters as his mother stood, pale and

8

quiet, by the door. He did not understand much, but he knew that everyone was unhappy. As John watched, two men took his father away to Lincoln Castle to be locked up in the debtors' prison because he could not pay back the money that he owed.

But this time passed. There were good people in the town, who helped their minister's family. After a while the debt was paid, and Samuel Wesley returned home.

As John grew older he wandered around the village and the fields. He watched farmers driving bawling cattle and squealing pigs to market in Epworth. On the road he saw a highwayman pelting fast behind a beplumed gentleman who spurred his horse to reach the town and safety. He wandered about the quiet churchyard with his sister Hetty, and she read to him the names on the old stones. He sat by the fire and listened to his mother talking of that faraway wilderness called America, where heathen savages roamed the forests. He heard his father speak of Queen Anne, in her fine palaces in London. And he listened to his older brother's letters, telling of the Latin and Greek that he was learning.

Susanna Wesley set aside one hour a week for a quiet time alone with each child. In this hour she talked to her children about religion, and answered their questions. John's night was Thursday, and he looked forward to it eagerly all week.

After Anne there was another little sister, who died. And after that came Charles, followed by a baby named Kezia. Kezia was the youngest in the family—the last child to be born to Susanna and Samuel Wesley.

BIRTHDAY

John opened his eyes very early on his fifth birthday morning. It was so early that the sun was not yet up. The gray light that comes before dawn was like a soft mist in the nursery, which was up under the thatched roof of the cottage. John felt confused at first. As his ears awakened, he heard Nurse snoring harshly, and then the light feet of mice scurrying around in the storeroom below. Father was doing better with his crops now, and there was wheat and flour there.

John pushed himself up on one elbow and looked around. In here with him slept the nurse and all of the children except the two older girls. John's bed was next to the big chest under the window. As the room grew lighter, the girls began to awaken and the baby, Charles, to cry. Outside, birds were singing in the hawthorn tree.

Then John remembered. Suddenly a great wave of fear swept over him. Today was June 17. Today he was five years old. Today he was to learn to read. A fifth birthday in the Wesley house was not a day for candles and cake. It was the day when a child made his parents proud, or ashamed, of him.

Nurse got up and dressed herself and the baby. Then the older girls helped the younger, and they clattered down the stairs. John could smell oatmeal porridge and hot milk. He didn't move at once. In the doorway Nurse turned and spoke over the baby's head, "You, John, now get yourself up and into your clothes. Your mother will be waiting for you."

John crawled out from beneath the covers and dressed. When he reached the kitchen he sat down at the table quietly. On the long table were two big bowls of oatmeal porridge, and two big bowls of warm milk. Father and Mother were already there. After saying grace, Father dipped his spoon into the bowl of oatmeal, then raised it slowly to his mouth. Then he dipped into the bowl of milk, and into his mouth it went. After Father, the girls' spoons went in, one after the other. At the other end of the table Mother was dipping her spoon into her big bowl, followed by each child, according to age. John reached for the bowl in his turn, though he had small appetite for it today.

When the bowls were almost empty, with just enough left in them for two more servings, Father called out, "Hold! Enough!" Each child laid his spoon on the table and rose. Cook and Nurse must have their breakfast now.

"Go into the front room, Jack," said Mrs. Wesley with a smile. "I will come in as soon as I have fed the baby."

12

As he walked slowly into the front room, where the children had their lessons, John thought that today he had rather be in the village school. It was taught by a man who was ignorant and careless. "He wears his kindness on his knuckles," Susanna Wesley had declared. But it was not punishment that John feared. He was afraid that he would disappoint his father and mother.

He sat there, listening to the household noises. He heard Mother giving instructions and saying that she was not to be disturbed until evening. He heard the girls laughing and chattering at their tasks, and the baby gurgling to himself. He heard Nurse saying to Cook, "Every Wesley young one has learned letters in six hours, but two of the girls. Mistress Wesley thinks them dull."

"Why not use a hornbook, like others do? That's easier, they say. And I heard that one lady had her hornbook made of gingerbread, and that when the letters were in the head they were in the stomach too."

The servants laughed. John had seen a hornbook. It was a sheet of paper with letters printed on it, and sometimes a verse. This

14

was in a wooden frame with a handle, and the paper was covered with a sheet of horn, so thin that the letters showed through. He thought that this would probably be an easier way to learn. But his mother scorned the easy way. Her children were to be taught by her, strictly but patiently.

When Susanna Wesley entered the front room, her skirts were rustling briskly. She sat down at once and placed the sheet of letters before her small son.

"Now, John, this is the letter A. Study it well. . . . What is this letter, John?"

All day John studied his letters. At noon he and his mother had a short time in the kitchen for dinner. After dinner John studied, and his mother patiently told him the names of the letters, one at a time. As the day grew warmer, John could hear a bumble-bee buzzing endlessly around his bent head. But he kept his mind on his task. His spirits rose. He was doing well. When he looked up into his mother's face, he could see that. She was smiling with a proud look, not with the patient look that she had had at first.

By the middle of the afternoon John knew his letters. And he learned to read a little prayer as well.

The door opened and in came Father.

"Well, Susanna, how is this child doing? Can he learn to read as well as his brother Samuel and his sister Martha?"

"He has learned his letters, Samuel, and he knows a little prayer too. John is a bright boy."

Father patted John on the shoulder.

"That is a brave lad, Jack. You are not only bright, but you can work hard, too. . . . Susanna, I wonder at your patience in teaching these children. You will tell a child the same thing twenty times."

Susanna smiled at her husband.

"Had I satisfied myself with mentioning it only nineteen," she replied quietly, "I should have lost all my labor. For it was the twentieth time that crowned the whole."

FIRE!

One night John awoke to strange sounds in the cottage.

"Father!" his sister Hetty was screaming. "The house is afire! Help! Fire!"

John could hear the other girls calling, and the baby crying, and the old nurse shouting. He smelled the sour smoke and saw a queer reddish light in the nursery. There was a crackling noise, too, coming from the storeroom beneath. Up here, under the thatched roof, it was growing very hot.

John sat up. Quite suddenly he saw that the room was empty. He remembered now that the nurse had called frantically to him to hurry, as she herded the other children down the steep stairs. He had heard the wind blow the door shut with a bang. John felt dazed and his head hurt. But he got out of bed and tried to follow Nurse to the stairs. As he pulled the nursery door open, flames swept into the room. The hall outside was ablaze, and he could not get to the stairs. He pushed the door shut again with all of his strength. Gasping, he stumbled across to the window. This was a small opening overhung by the straw of the roof. John pushed and pushed at the window. At last it swung open.

Below, in the garden, John saw a group of neighbors. They were crying and shouting, and running about with leather buckets. His father stood there, counting his children, all shivering in their nightgowns and caps. Their pale faces were lighted by the glowing cottage. John called out, but no one heard him.

"Susanna," he heard his father cry, "I do not see John."

Mrs. Wesley grasped Nurse by the arm. "Where is John?"

The nurse, shaking as in a fit, cried, "I woke the girls when I heard Hetty screaming. I snatched up the baby and called to John to come. I thought he was right behind me. Alas! Where is he?" She fell on her knees, praying loudly.

Mrs. Wesley turned around and tried to rush into the flaming cottage. Two men pulled her back. No one could get up the burning stairs. The thatch was breaking into fire, first here and then there. Large pieces were being blown down by the wind.

Just then Susanna heard her husband cry, "Look! There is John!"

She ran back to the garden and saw her husband point upward to the little nursery window. There was John, kneeling on the big chest.

"See!" shouted Mr. Wesley hoarsely. "Thank God, he is still alive!"

He tried to reach up to John, but could not. He dropped on his knees to pray. A farmer's boy called to a man nearby, "Here-ee, there — take me on your shoulders. I will reach down the child."

The man stood with legs apart, braced, and stooped over. The boy climbed on the man's shoulders and put his arms up. Once he fell, but soon got up again.

"Climb out, John," shouted Mrs. Wesley, "Climb out!"

John crawled into the window and leaned far down. The boy grasped him under the arms and lowered him safely into the hands of people below.

Samuel Wesley took his son, and then Susanna held him close. The minister called his neighbors to him. As the flaming roof of the cottage collapsed, they all dropped down on their knees.

"Come, neighbors, let us thank God!" said Mr. Wesley. "John has been snatched as a brand from the burning. God has given me all my children. Let the house go. I am rich enough."

Next day the family stood sadly looking at the pile of hot ashes and stones that had been their home. John heard a woman ask, "How did the fire start, do you think? I heard just now that it was set by those same ruffians who have tormented our minister before."

"Aye, so they say, and I think with truth," said a friend, frowning. "You remember last year, how rascals set fire to the Wesley fields, and burned all of the flax? And then the terrible night when the church was broken into, and the Bible torn in pieces and strewn about the ground?"

"That I do! Our parson be a good man. But you know there are some hereabouts who hate the church and all it stands for."

The year that followed the fire was a hard one for the Wesley family. They had no home, and very little money. Mr. Wesley wondered sadly how any human being could set fire to a cottage filled with innocent children. But he did not condemn anyone. Friends in the village took the Wesleys in, a few children in each household. Mrs. Wesley grieved at the parceling out of the family and the separation of the children. She said to her husband, "I do worry much about our children. I have tried to teach them decent ways and manners, and the right things always. Yet now that they are not in my care I fear that much of my training is lost."

"Do not grieve, wife," said her husband. "We will build our new house where the old one stood, and it will be a larger and a

better home. You will soon have your brood under your wing again."

But when the children were happily home, their mother was shocked at the manners and ways that they had picked up in the other houses. "Indeed," she said, with her most disapproving look, "they have taken on a clownish accent and many rude ways."

When the family gathered in their new house for the first time, Samuel Wesley brought in a charred stick of wood from the old burned cottage. As his wife and children watched, he hung it inside the front door. This was to remind them all to be thankful for their new home. John and his younger brother Charles, and the sisters, were glad to be in the new house. No longer did they have to eat in the kitchen as they had done in the cottage. Here they had a dining room. Here, too, they had more bedrooms upstairs, and even an attic. And the roof was of tile, and not of straw.

Yet so poor was the minister that for many years after the house was finished, there was not enough furniture in it for comfort. As for food, Mrs. Wesley said that getting bread for her table was such a task that she sometimes had no appetite for it when she got it.

John was a quiet boy. He worked hard and said little. He thought so long before making a decision, and gave his reasons at such length, that his father was amazed at him. He said to him once, "Child, you think to carry everything by dint of argument; but you will find later how little is ever done in this world by that means."

When John was about nine, he and four of the other children caught the dreaded smallpox. Mr. Wesley was in London attend-

ing to church affairs. Nursing her brood kept Susanna Wesley busy day and night. Yet she found time to write to her husband, to tell him of the children. Some of them complained, for the pox was painful and they suffered severely. But of John she wrote: "Jack has borne his disease bravely, like a man, and indeed like a Christian, without any complaint, though he seemed angry at the smallpox when they were sore, as we guessed by his looking sourly at them, for he never said anything."

That year something far more important than smallpox happened to John. His father was in London again. His mother became weary of the dull sermons of the curate, who preached of nothing but paying one's debts. She was excited by news of two Danish missionaries and their work in the East Indies. She felt that her family needed more than they were getting from the curate's sermons. So she began to hold little meetings on Sunday afternoons in her kitchen. At these meetings she told the servants and her children of the work of the missionaries.

Others heard of the meetings and asked to come. At last so many people came to the house that there was scarcely room for them. The meetings shocked Mr. Wesley's assistant, the curate.

23

Religious meetings outside the church were unheard of. But when the curate wrote to Mr. Wesley in London, Samuel did not forbid the meetings, though he wrote to Susanna that he really did not approve.

John, and his little brother Charles, always remembered the meetings in the big kitchen. It was because of these gatherings, as well as the thorough religious training that she gave her boys, that Susanna Wesley was later to be called "the mother of Methodism."

OFF TO LONDON

It was a great day for John when, at eleven years old, he said good-by to his mother, his little brother, and his sisters, and set off for London. John climbed up behind his father on the family horse, which trotted off to Lincoln. He sat holding onto his father, his eyes bright with excitement. His older brother Samuel was now a teacher at Westminster School. But Mr. Wesley had no money to send John to school there. For some worried months Mr. and Mrs. Wesley had feared that Jack could not continue his education. Then a wealthy friend, Lord Buckingham, arranged for young John to receive a free scholarship to Charterhouse School. In the town of Lincoln John and his father left the horse to be taken back to Epworth, and got into the London stagecoach.

This was the year 1714. It was a time of change for England. Queen Anne had died in August, and her cousin George I, Elector

of Hanover, had come to the throne. Queen Anne had been a religious woman. She had agreed to have George as her successor only because he was a Protestant. George I was a German, who could speak no English. He spent much of his time in Germany, leaving the affairs of the government to ministers and the cabinet. Scotland and Ireland had joined with England to become the United Kingdom. Peace had been gained after a war with France.

Everything was new to John as he traveled to London. As the stagecoach rattled along the rough road, he could not take his eyes from the hills and hedges, the fields and streams flashing by. When they came within sight of a village or town, the horn gave out a blast that echoed from the hills and brought dogs and children running into the streets. John caught his breath and clutched the seat as the driver pulled up with a flourish before each inn at which they stopped. And then his breath leaped out in a gasp as they started up again, horn blowing, dogs barking.

They went through the small towns which were growing up all about outside the old London walls. Then the coach rolled through the city gates and a roar of sound hit their ears.

Hawkers cried their wares: "Fish!" "Bread!" "Plum puddings!" "Firewood!"

John saw beggars grasping at the coats of travelers as they left the coach. Rich dandies were stepping into sedan chairs to avoid the mud of the narrow streets. The smells and sights and uproar were staggering to the boy from Epworth.

As they came to the Charterhouse School, John looked eagerly about him. Charterhouse was an old group of buildings, built around a courtyard. It had been constructed many years before by monks, and had later been bought as a castle by the Duke of Norfolk. In 1611, Charterhouse had become a school for the sons of teachers and ministers and other educated men who did not have enough money to pay their children's schooling. It was also a home for old army and navy men, called pensioners.

John looked up at the thick stone walls and gray towers and thought it more like a castle prison. As he and his father walked across the courtyard into the rooms of the headmaster, John's ears caught the sound of shouting and laughing on the green. But when he told his father good-by, he felt lost and lonely. One of the younger masters took him to the green where the boys were playing. There John stood stiffly, straining his ears to catch the sound of his father's departing footsteps.

Charterhouse was a strange world to John. It took some getting used to, especially when he saw how the other boys behaved. When the bell clanged its brassy call to rise, the others

28

turned over for just one more wink of sleep in their warm cots in the dormitory room upstairs. But John had been taught otherwise. He got up at once, shivered himself into his clothes, and flung his school gown about him. Then he clattered down the stairs and out through a stone passage to the field. Here he ran around the green three times, as his father had told him that he must do, for the sake of his health.

When the other gown boys, in their long robes with the pointed sleeves and silver-buckled shoes, dashed to the wash trough, John was already there. He was clean and damp, and had been first to use the one roller towel. But this habit of doing things on time did nothing for him at table. The senior boys, big and tough, always took the meat from smaller fellows. For years, said John Wesley, he lived chiefly on bread and vegetables. All he ever got was the smell of roast meat.

John had to run errands for the big boys, to come running to them when they shouted "Fag!" and to submit to their tormenting ways without protest.

The days were long periods of study. In the big room the

older boys had a fireplace at one side, and the younger boys one at the other. But John was often called away from his writing table to get coals for the fire for the big boys. When he returned to his place, he had to stare hard at his pounce pot of blotting sand, as he dipped quill into the thick ink and tried to get his thoughts back on study.

John studied and worked hard. His older brother Samuel came to see him and reported to their father: "Jack is a brave boy, learning Hebrew as fast as he can."

In one corner of the writing room was a high stool. Here a lazy boy who had not done his work had to perch, wearing a big false face with "Dunce" written across it. John never had to sit on that stool. He was interested in his study of Latin, Greek, Hebrew, and Philosophy. He studied Mathematics, too, although this subject was not looked on with respect by most of the teachers. The masters required that Latin be spoken in the classrooms and even on the playing green. English, they despised as a vulgar tongue.

For amusement the students played at tennis, a simple cricket game, and with marbles, kites, and battledores. A favorite game of the younger boys was a fast slide down the banisters to the first floor, when no master was around to catch them.

John did not like the ways of many of the older fellows. This was a time when cockfights, bearbaitings, and other cruel sports were indulged in throughout the city. These older boys often went to such fights, betting and drinking. Yet there were others, like John, who were quiet and studious. And the walls of the old school seemed to hold within them the childhood memories of former Charterhouse boys who had left to become famous literary men, scholars, and bishops.

Late one day Mr. Tooke, a young teacher, noticed that the smaller boys were not in the playground. He went to the long dark writing room. There he saw a group of boys listening eagerly to a story being quietly told to them by John Wesley, Mr. Tooke stood until the story was ended. Then he said with a smile, "I had thought to find these boys in some mischief. But you talk well to them, Wesley. You may do so again, whenever you find the time."

While John was still at Charterhouse, his younger brother Charles came up to London to enter Westminster School, not far away. This was a joy to the three brothers, for now they could see each other from time to time.

John was well thought of at Charterhouse. He was a hard worker and a quiet, orderly student. Yet he had the same independence that had made his grandfather and great-grandfather willing to suffer persecution and arrest for not following the strict rules of the Church of England. He was already thinking seriously of his future, too. He loved the work with books that went with

32

a university life, and thought that he probably could become a teacher. Yet he had grown up in a family where the men had all become clergymen, and where he had been taught to think first of religion.

As he reached his seventeenth year he thought often of becoming a minister and began to consider entering Oxford University. He knew that because of his good work at Charterhouse he would receive a scholarship at the University.

"I wish you to call on Dr. Sacheverell," wrote Mr. Wesley to John, not long before he was to leave Charterhouse, "and get a letter of introduction for the college." So John went to see the famous scholar, friend of his father.

"But," said John later to Charles, "when I was introduced I found him alone, as tall as a Maypole, and as fine as an archbishop."

"How do you do, young Mr. Wesley," boomed the doctor.

34

"And so your father says that you are going to Oxford?" He frowned at the thin youth, who was no bigger than a boy of fourteen. "You are too young to go to the University. You cannot .possibly know Greek and Latin yet. Go back to school!"

John answered politely, "Good day, sir," but he looked up at the pompous doctor as David looked at Goliath, and despised him.

As he walked quietly back to Charterhouse, to pack his few threadbare belongings, John thought, "If I do not know Greek and Latin better than you, I ought to go back to school indeed. And nothing on earth could make me go to see you again."

STEER STEADY

Oxford University was the center of student life for all England. The ancient stone buildings on the River Cherwell were a gathering place for the sons of the wealthy. Many of them came to play and not to study. But there were others who wanted to learn Latin, Greek, and Philosophy. Some were serious young men who were sons of clergymen and who came with scholarships. John Wesley was one of these.

He arrived with a few well-worn clothes, dark and of a simple cut, and an allowance of forty pounds a year as a former Charterhouse scholar. He brought with him also a love for languages, and for learning, and a friendly spirit. John Wesley was only five feet, four inches tall. He was so thin and small that at first few noticed him. But it was not long until other students came to know and

like him for his wit, his poetic gifts in writing, and for his steady, clear mind.

But John was often troubled, for he had so little money that he was sometimes in debt for books or other necessities. His father could not help him much.

Once John wrote jokingly to his mother that the town was filled with thieves and cutpurses, so that it was not safe to be in the streets. "A gentleman whom I know was standing at the door of a coffeehouse about seven last evening. When he turned around, his cap and wig were snatched off his head, and though he followed the thief to a considerable distance he was unable to recover them. I am pretty safe from such bandits, for unless they carried me away, carcass and all, they would have but a poor purchase."

At Oxford John was frequently tired. He was used to long hours of work, and little food. Yet now he felt weary and was worried by a cough that would not leave him. As he climbed the stairs to his room in Christ Church College each day, he felt that he did not have the physical strength to do all that he wanted to do. And then he found a book on a bookstall. It was Dr. Cheyne's *Book of Health and Long Life.*

John bought this book and set about studying it. He knew that many men died of tuberculosis at an early age, and that he was likely to go that way himself if his health did not improve. So now he determined to follow this book. He would eat sparingly and drink nothing but water. This should be easy, since he had little money for food and drink anyway. But he would also spend much time out of doors. He would walk in the open air in every spare moment. And he would swim in the river on every warm day.

When John had been at Oxford several years, Charles arrived from Westminster School to enroll as a student. The brothers did not care for rowdy friends, and both were seriously interested in religion and study. Before long the Wesley brothers had collected about them a few others. They held meetings to try to improve their minds by study and discussion.

About that time John decided what his life was to be. He had long thought of it, and for some time had considered becoming a teacher. But now he made up his mind to become a minister.

So he was ordained as a minister of the Church of England, and preached his first sermon at South Lye. But he did not think that his study was ended. John wanted to get a fellowship at Lincoln College, Oxford. A fellowship would pay him for teaching while he continued his studies. He asked his father to help him with any advice or by an appeal to any friend who might put in a word for him. John knew that there were some at the University who did not want him to get the fellowship, for they thought him too serious and too critical of the ways of others.

Old Samuel Wesley, who was again in debt, managed somehow to send John what he needed, and to help by writing to friends. And John received the fellowship. But he determined to do everything possible to save money. He even let his hair grow long so that he would not have to spend anything at the barber's.

John still wrote poetry at Lincoln College, and Charles also was known for his poetry. John was getting a reputation as well for his great skill in answering questions on religion and scholarly subjects. He was growing more and more determined to help people. To do this he must have more time. How could he have more? He was a believer in leading a methodical life. Already he regulated his time carefully. Now he decided to account for every minute. And he said to Charles, "Leisure and I have taken leave of one another, and I propose to be busy as long as I live."

Every duty had a time, and he was on time for every duty. John never took a vacation from this rule. He worked out a system of early rising. Each morning he got up an hour earlier until he found the exact amount of sleep that was necessary for him. And from then on he never had more. He trained himself to sleep on

a hard bed. He rose at four each day, in the darkness, well before dawn. The extra hour or two before his duties began he used for writing in his diaries and journals, which he kept continuously.

John Wesley was a man who trained his mind well. But he was also a man of action. He wanted to practice all that he preached. Even though still a student he wanted more and more to help others. How could he do this? He could deny himself every luxury, so that he could give small sums of money to aid the poor. But that was not enough. All about him were dirt and poverty and ignorance. People high and low cared nothing for goodness and mercy and spiritual growth. How the rich drank brandy and gambled and took part in cruel sports! How the poor drank gin and fought and robbed! Little children were forced to work at five years old and were taught nothing. John Wesley saw these things and felt that he must find a better way to help people.

Perhaps he could help his father? Not long before, John had

received a letter from the Reverend Samuel Wesley asking him to come home to Epworth and be his assistant. John did not want to leave Oxford. He liked to teach Greek and to go out of a Sunday to preach in towns and villages nearby. But his father, now grown old, was having a hard time. He had to preach in the village of Wroote, about five miles from Epworth, as well as in Epworth. Wroote was a savage and wild place. It was so hard to get to, across streams and bogs, that folk called it "Wroote-out-of-England." Not long since, the old minister had nearly lost his life when his boat had sunk in a bog near there. There were many such remote villages in England, where people had never even seen a cart. They carried their few goods on their backs. And they walked through bogs on long wooden stilts.

So John got a two-year leave of absence from Oxford and went to live in the village of Wroote. These years were not pleasant for him. He missed the friendship of other young students at Oxford, and he found no chance to help these people. They resented him, and would not change their wild ways.

John could not see that he was helping the country people, so when his two years were over he was glad to return to Oxford. There he found that Charles had gotten together the few serious men who were interested in religion. They had formed a study group which other students scornfully called the Holy Club. They wanted to worship as well as study together. John joined them at once, and before long became their leader. He taught them his methodical ways of study and work, and so they came to be called "Methodists." This was a joke to those gay young students who laughed at serious ideas. But it was not a joke to the Methodists.

There was a young man in their group named Morgan. He coughed a great deal, and his hands were so white and thin that one could almost see through them. Morgan thought much of the prisoners in the castle jail, and wanted to do something to relieve their misery. Here was something that John, too, could do. It was something that the members of the Holy Club all could do. On his father's advice John asked permission of the bishop's chaplain. Having received it, John organized trips to the prison.

"Going to prison?" jeered the young dandies.

One of them placed his jaunty hands behind him and stalked along, imitating the members of the Holy Club. "See the Methodists! Going to see their friends, the jailbirds!"

But the members of the Holy Club said nothing. They went to the prison. As they came near, their eyes caught the dark frown of the high walls. And their noses stiffened at the foul smells. High above them in the air wheeled glistening wings of birds, free to move where they willed. The footsteps of the young men echoed on the damp stone steps behind the jailer. At first the

43

prisoners greeted them with oaths and cries and groans.

As the five young men walked among the prisoners, lying in the straw, the ragged men and women fell silent. They stared at the visitors with surprise. Why had they come here? Why would anyone come down here from the sweet fresh air? Prisons were crowded with criminals, the insane, and men who could not pay their debts, all thrown in together.

The Holy Club could not do much. But the sympathy of the young men for the prisoners was something new and wonderful to the unfortunates.

The Oxford students seemed to enjoy making fun of the Holy Club. When John wrote his father of this, Mr. Wesley replied: "I question whether a mortal can arrive to a greater degree of perfection than steadily to do good, and for that very reason patiently and meekly to suffer evil. Bear no more sail than is necessary, but steer steady."

John did not forget that. He tried to "steer steady." He and his brother Charles were saddened when their friend Morgan, who had gone home to Ireland, died of tuberculosis. But they continued to try to help the prisoners.

John and Charles tried to interest more students in joining the Holy Club, but without much success. They slowly made a few more friends for the Club, and these friends gave money to their charity fund. The money was used to buy medicines for the sick, to pay small debts to release prisoners, and to buy books. John cut down all of his expenses to a bare living, in order to add to these funds. And when he could save no more, he took his few pictures from his walls and sold them.

THE ROAD HOME

When John had lived at Oxford for nearly ten years he began to think often of Epworth. It had been long since he and Charles had visited there. He could close his eyes and seem to smell the musky odor of the thatched roof of their early home and the clean, washed smell of dawn on wet leaves. Now, as he sat and heard the tap-tapping of a finger of green ivy on his window, he knew that summer was near. A door downstairs slammed shut and he heard the quick steps of Charles on the way up. John smiled and rose to greet him.

Charles sat down by the window. Together they stared at the sprig of ivy, which seemed to call to them to come out.

"I will make a guess as to your thoughts, Charles," smiled John. "They are home in Epworth, aren't they?"

Charles looked startled. "Yes, brother, but how did you know?"

"Mine are there, too. Perhaps it is the warm wind. Perhaps it is the letters we have had of late. Kezia writes that Father is not so well now."

"If we could go home for a few days?"

"Why not?"

Charles held out his empty hands, palms up. "Without coach fare? How could we? We have no horses, you know."

John smiled again. "Then we will walk." He laughed outright at his brother's look of amazement.

"Have you forgotten that Epworth is beyond a hundred miles from here?"

"We can do it."

Charles went to make up a small bundle of a few necessities. He knew that if John said they could do it, they could.

The brothers set out. Roads were scarcely more than tracks, rutted with holes, often filled with stones and water. Fine coaches and horsemen galloped past, scattering them with mud. But Charles laughed, and John suggested that they try two things. They would speak nothing but Latin, for practice, and they would attempt to read while walking the two books they had brought. This was no easy matter. Once John, with his eyes on a book, stepped into a muddy hole to the knees. After that, the one who was reading aloud walked just behind the other, to keep from falling.

The two brothers grew used to tramping as much as twenty-five miles a day. As they neared the village of Epworth their steps were brisk and they smiled at each other. There was the shop of

47

the butcher. And there was the old cloakmaker behind his little green-glass window. There was the quiet church, surrounded by its graves. And there was the Wesley parsonage, not so new now as when they had left it, somehow looking smaller than they remembered it. No straw thatch was on the roof, to risk a fire, but John smiled when he saw that a small brown bird had built her nest in the vines climbing above the windows. Perhaps this was of the same family of birds that had so annoyed the Reverend Wesley by building in the thatch of the old cottage?

Home was the same, and yet different. John noticed at once that his father's step was slower, his shoulders more bowed, and that he put one gnarled hand on his heart when he moved quickly. But Mr. Wesley had an eye as keen and a mind as alert for knowledge and for good works as ever. Mrs. Wesley still walked erectly and spoke with the old authority. Her hair showed gray under the ruffle of her neat cap. John and Charles saw the light of pleasure come into her face as she welcomed her sons home again.

Susanna, Emilia, and Kezia were here. Anne had died some years before. Mary, who was an invalid, lived at Wroote with her husband, the pastor, John Whitelamb. Hetty had left home when she married. Martha was now Mrs. Hall, living in London. There her gift for poetry had made her a friend of the famous Dr. Samuel Johnson. Susanna was back with her parents, after an unfortunate marriage that had not lasted.

Charles frowned at John as he saw that there was so little bread that their mother had not taken any. But he said nothing about it. And he and John brought smiles to their parents' faces with talk of Oxford, the Holy Club, and the friendship of another

48

young minister, George Whitefield, a member of their group.

Supper over, the family arose. But before they could reach the door, the latch flew up, and the door slowly opened a crack. Kezia jumped back and shrieked, "That is Jeffrey! See!"

John stepped forward and flung the door wider open. But the hallway was empty. He smiled at Kezia. "Look here, sister. This Jeffrey? Is he the same mysterious ghost that you wrote about when I was at Charterhouse, when you were a little girl?"

"Yes, Jeffrey is our ghost, Jack. He lives in the attic."

"Nonsense, Kezia, you don't really believe that, do you?"

But, on looking about him, John saw the family glancing uneasily at one another. He was a little disturbed himself during family prayers. As the old minister prayed, there were queer raps and knockings. They seemed to come from the table. Or was it the door? As soon as he got up from his knees, John went to look into the hall again. He found it as empty as before.

During their short stay both Charles and John wondered at

their sisters. This was a lonely place for girls who had received an education. And the girls were so poor that they could not leave. They had to wear made-over clothes. By the time Kezia got a dress it had been worn by three or four others for years. Perhaps they entertained themselves imagining Jeffrey? If so, they did a good job of it. John, sitting quietly reading, would hear the door bang and see Susanna holding it stubbornly with her shoulder.

"It's Jeffrey," she said firmly, "and I shall not let him in."

John shook his head, but half believed in the ghost, too.

When John and Charles returned to Oxford, John was offered a place as assistant minister eight miles away. Now he became a preacher who rode from place to place on horseback. Farmers plodding the road got used to seeing the small thin man, on a slow horse, reading a book as he rode. Always in his saddlebags he carried books. After a while he began to translate foreign books into English. In his sermons he shared what he learned with the people. He also shared his books with them, when they could read them.

To be good, a man must understand, and to understand he must read.

Old Samuel Wesley was growing weaker. He wished to have John take his place in Epworth. John considered this, and his older brother, Samuel, advised him to do it. John was coughing again, and was losing weight. One day as he rode beside a stream he felt a rush of blood from his mouth. This meant the dreaded disease, tuberculosis. He dismounted from his horse and plunged into the cold stream to stop the blood. What should he do? Life would be easier for him at Epworth, but he felt that his gifts did not belong in so small a place. As he rode on, he decided that he would not go to Epworth.

In 1735 Samuel Wesley died. Susanna Wesley left the parsonage to live with her daughters, first one and then another. Brother Samuel was married and was teaching in London. At Oxford, John and Charles often talked of what they wanted to do. They remembered the stories their mother had told of the wonderful work of the Danish missionaries. Their thoughts turned toward

such work. They listened eagerly to the tales of the American wilderness that were spreading in England.

Colonel Oglethorpe, who had already taken two shiploads of debtors from the prisons to his colony in Georgia, was back in England. John and Charles heard of the Indian chief who had come with him. The Wesley brothers talked of going to Georgia as missionaries to preach to the Indians. John's health was much improved. His outdoor life, and his regular way of living, had cured him of tuberculosis. His cough had left him, and he felt ready for new undertakings. He found that the Society for the Propagation of the Gospel in Foreign Parts would send him to Georgia. And Charles was promised a position as secretary to Colonel Oglethorpe.

The brothers worried about their mother. How would she take such news? They went to see her, to tell her that they were soon to sail to America. Her eyes lighted with pride, and the staunch old lady, as commanding as ever, said, "Had I twenty sons, I should rejoice if they were all so employed."

IN OTHER LANDS

On a clear October day, in 1735, John and Charles Wesley boarded a little sailing vessel bound for the colony of Georgia. They were going with a company of immigrants from debtors' prisons. On the ship also was a group of Germans who belonged to a religious order called Moravians.

The boat had no sooner sailed than Charles began to get together a small class among the children. John started to teach English to the Moravians. At the same time he learned German from them. He could already speak Latin, French, and Italian.

The voyage was a long one across stormy seas. In January they sailed into the outskirts of a hurricane. Many were ill from the pounding of the waves and the tossing of the vessel. John, who was not seasick, went among the passengers and helped them all he could. He wrote in his journal:

"The waves of the sea were mighty, and raged horribly. The winds roared about and whistled as distinctly as a human voice. Every ten minutes came a shock against the stern or side of the ship, which one would think should dash the planks in pieces."

He admired the calm faith of the Moravians. Even the tiniest German children seemed not to be afraid. John made friends with the children as he learned their language. After the storms died down he spent much time talking and singing with them.

At the end of a long four months the little ship came to the shores of Georgia and sailed into the harbor of Savannah. The weary passengers went ashore to build their homes and make a new life.

Savannah was a small town facing the Savannah River, with the great unbroken forests of wild America at its back. From the settlement pioneers were going out into the wilderness to clear land and fight Indians, and to make farms with the labor of their hands. A few men were already owners of large plantations in the colony.

Charles Wesley took up his secretarial work. John Wesley found that he had been appointed the official pastor of the colony. This prevented him from carrying out his plan of going into the forests to work with the Indians. He was disturbed also that when the well-to-do people of the colony came to hear him preach they were dressed as fancily as the gay upper classes in London.

John Wesley was a young man strong in his beliefs. He had not yet learned any tolerance of the faults of others. He preached sternly against frivolity, and made many enemies by doing so. Both of the Wesleys went to the smaller villages near Savannah to preach, but everywhere they met opposition and were able to accomplish nothing with the adults.

But John Wesley always made friends with children. Now he and Charles Delamotte, the friend who had accompanied them to the colony, thought that they could educate the children of Savannah. They started the first Sunday school. One morning Mr. Delamotte told John Wesley that the poorer children were no longer attending the school. He thought this was because the richer boys made fun of them for not wearing shoes.

John Wesley thought for a moment. Then he said quietly, "I will teach the class today."

He sat down and took off his shoes and hose. Then, calmly and with great dignity, he walked barefooted to the school and into the little room where the boys were scuffling and shouting. He stood silently until the room was quiet, and then commenced the day's work. The boys stared in amazement at his bare feet.

"Look," they whispered, "the parson is barefoot!"

Every Sunday their teacher appeared with his feet bare, but said nothing about it. After a while the boys became more serious and seemed ashamed of their cruel behavior. The pupils who had no shoes came back. And before long some of the boys requested to be admitted to communion.

After a few months Charles went back to England. John spoke so sternly in his sermons that those he offended began to plot against him. Once he refused to admit a wealthy young woman to communion. Her uncle, the chief magistrate of Savannah, brought the minister to public trial and refused to let him answer the charges. Wesley felt that his trip to America had been a failure. He decided sadly that he should return to England.

When he stepped ashore again in his own land he felt that

he had not had enough faith and that he himself, for all his trials, had never been a really good Christian. He realized that he had been too concerned with saving his own soul and had not had enough understanding of others.

One of the fine things that John recorded in his journal as a result of his trip to America was his friendship with the German Moravians. In London he met three of them and traveled to Oxford with them. He found them interesting, although he could not agree with their religious views. At Oxford John preached to a large group of prisoners at the Castle. Here he began his work once more in England, in the same place where he had begun to preach.

One evening a friend asked John to go to St. Paul's Cathedral. There he heard the anthem, "Out of the deep have I called unto Thee, O Lord." That evening he visited a religious society meeting. During the reading of Luther's preface to the Epistle to the Romans he felt that his heart was strangely warmed, and that he did believe completely.

Charles wrote in his journal of that night: "Towards ten my brother was brought in triumph by a troop of friends, and declared, 'I believe.' We sang the hymn with great joy and parted with prayer." The hymn was one Charles had written the previous day.

John Wesley wished to know more about the Moravians. He had been told of the two settlements they had founded at Marienborn and at Herrnhut. Now he decided to make the journey into Germany to visit these communities.

He first paid his mother a visit at Salisbury, where she was staying with one of her daughters. Then he joined a group of English and German travelers who were also going to see the Moravian communities. It was no easy matter to travel on the continent of Europe then. Innkeepers were suspicious of men dressed in sober cloth, and often refused them a night's lodging. But the travelers were entertained by friends in Holland. There they admired the clean streets, the neat dress of the people, and the canals bordered by trees.

They went on foot through the Dutch country and into Germany. At Cologne they took a boat up the Rhine. The serious-mannered men from England were much amazed at the Lutherans, who ended their Sunday with dancing to the music of fiddles. And they saw the Roman Catholics worshiping singly, kneeling before images in shrines.

The voyage up the Rhine was peaceful and beautiful. The little vessel was pulled by horses on a towing path, and moved slowly. Inside the boat the passengers sat, gazing up at the steep mountains, wooded to the tops. Here and there a monastery or castle frowned down on the green Rhine waters. Near Frankfurt

60

they got off, weary from the journey. They were surprised to find themselves halted at the city gates. The guard refused to let them in, for they had no passes. Then John Wesley remembered that the father of one of his Moravian friends in England lived here. He sent word to Mr. Böhler, who came at once, took them into the city, and to his home. Here he entertained them until they were rested and ready to go on to Herrnhut.

They started to walk across Germany, with its neat farms and old cities. But many times they had to find a dirty, dark little inn in a village because the larger towns would not let them in. They passed through the busy cities of Leipzig and Dresden and journeyed up the Elbe River. At last they came to Herrnhut. Here they were welcomed into the little community and remained for some weeks.

The religious settlement of Herrnhut was located on the edge of Bohemia. It was a lovely little village, surrounded by gardens and forests. The brethren worked together in the fields for the benefit of the whole community, and led simple, devout

62

lives. The village had a school, a church, and a hall in a building called the Orphan House. The group of children looked clean and happy. What a fine thing such an orphan house would be in England! John thought. How peaceful and how useful was the life of this place!

John Wesley wished to stay a long time. But he knew that he had work to do in his own country. So he told his friends in Herrnhut good-by and returned as he had come, on foot, to Rotterdam, where he took ship for England.

COME TO THE FIELDS

One evening John Wesley walked through the London streets to a meeting of Methodists. His eyes were on the rowdy people. Overhead huge signs swung out above the streets, which were as narrow as passageways. In London, instead of a number, each house had a name and a sign—The Blue Boar, The Armored Horse, or The Rollicking Pig. Only a man as small as John Wesley could walk along without cracking his head on them.

It was not really safe to walk the London streets, even for a minister in his sober clothing. Already gin shops were filling with drunken men and shouting women. Already tough street urchins were fighting in the filth flung from house windows. The terrible Mohawks, however, were not yet out. These were young dandies who amused themselves by cruel torture of men and women in the streets at night.

"Truly," thought John Wesley, as he looked about him, "truly the people, both high and low, could not be more depraved than they are now."

For some months after his return to England John Wesley, with his brother Charles, had been busy organizing Methodist Societies. These had been formed to enable a few religious folk in London to pray and sing hymns and help each other. Such a group met at a shop called "The Bible and Sun," in Wild Street. As their numbers grew, they moved to a room in Fetter Lane. The leaders of the societies who were most earnest in their work and able in organizing were later appointed by John Wesley as lay pastors. The societies formed classes to read good books and to help those in need. Members were expected to give a penny a week to the upkeep of the society, and share in all the work.

John's thoughts turned to a letter that he had received that day from his Oxford friend, George Whitefield. Whitefield had been refused the use of churches and was now preaching out of doors. The first time that Whitefield preached outside a church, near Bristol, people had flocked to hear him. He continued to hold meetings in the open for six weeks. Then he wrote asking John Wesley to take his place, for he wished to start preaching in another town.

John felt troubled. He was an ordained minister of the Church of England. He had no wish to start a new church. But only a few churches were open to Methodists. John was very busy in London, preaching in several churches. He wrote to George Whitefield that at Islington, when he left the church, "the fields, after service, were white with people praising God."

This small man, in his black clothes, frowned as he picked his

way carefully among the wild street gangs to Fetter Lane. It was a hard decision to make. He was thinking: I can scarcely reconcile myself to this strange way of preaching in the fields. I would think the saving of souls almost a sin if not done in church. But he remembered how Jesus had preached the Sermon on the Mount. And when he reached the door at Fetter Lane he had decided to go to Bristol, if the Society approved, and preach in the open.

On March 31 he met Whitefield in Bristol. That first time John Wesley spoke outdoors to three thousand people. He remained in Bristol until June, preaching to growing crowds, organizing Methodist Societies, and reading prayers to inmates of prisons. He began to collect money to provide a building in Bristol for the services and the societies. This was to be a place in the Horse Fair, with a chapel and meeting rooms, and it was to become a permanent meeting place for Methodists.

When John went back to London he found the room in Fetter Lane too small. So he borrowed money from a friend to repair an old deserted cannon foundry. At the Foundry, as the place was afterward called, he established the London headquarters for Methodism.

Methodist Societies were being formed in all parts of London, and John Wesley soon was riding his horse to distant towns to preach. He was sorry that his friend George Whitefield had decided to leave the Methodist group and join the Calvinists. Two of his other friends had gone with the German Moravians. But his brother Charles was always a good companion. Charles often traveled with John. He, also, took an active share of the work of the Methodist Societies, and preached in the open frequently.

66

Charles Wesley had a talent for powerful preaching, as well as for writing beautiful hymns.

In 1742 John Wesley went to preach to the miners. He was always concerned not only with religious services but with trying to improve lawless conditions. People were so dishonest at voting time that elections were jokes to them. Smuggling was so much practiced on the coasts that it was thought an ordinary job. John Wesley spoke against dishonesty and smuggling. This caused some to leave the Methodist Societies. But then better men and women came to join. Everywhere Methodism was creating better citizens, and turning them from violence.

John Wesley went to the mining town of Newcastle to visit a dying friend. There he saw the worst conditions of any place he had been. Nobody seemed interested in hearing a sermon.

At seven in the morning John Wesley rose and went into the streets of the town. He walked to Sandgate, in the poorest section, with his companion, John Taylor. Standing in the street they began to sing the Hundredth Psalm. A few frowsy people came out to see what the excitement was about. They stood listening. More came — until nearly fifteen hundred had gathered.

Wesley preached to them. That afternoon he preached again, and an immense crowd assembled.

None of these people had even imagined that a minister, or anyone else, would be interested in them. Now they begged Wesley to stay and talk with them.

This was a tiring visit for John Wesley, but he prepared to leave Newcastle with contentment in his heart. Never had he seen people more eager to hear him.

John Taylor was delayed in leaving, but said that he could catch up with Mr. Wesley. As John Wesley mounted his horse and jogged out through the town alone, he drew from his saddle-bag a worn copy of Shakespeare's plays to read along the road. Suddenly his horse shied. Wesley almost dropped his book. "Whoa, whoa there!"

He reached over to pat the horse's neck, and saw that there was a tiny child in the road. It was so thin that its bones seemed to thrust out through its skin. John Wesley dismounted and picked up the little one. He carried it to the roadside, where he saw a woman sitting beside an older child. The woman was white and shaking. Without a word he placed the child beside its mother. Then he went to his saddlebags. From them he drew all of the bread and meat that he had placed there for his day's food. He put it into the woman's hands. Then he took from his pocket some pills, which he laid on top of the food.

"Here," he said. "Divide the food among you, for you look starved. And then do you take these pellets, one at morning and one at night. They have aided in curing fevers before now. You have as bad an ague as I have ever seen. Can you get to your home?"

68

The woman looked up at him gratefully, and answered that she lived nearby, across the fields. The minister patted the children on their heads and blessed them. As he mounted his horse again he saw his companion riding toward him. As Taylor approached he said anxiously, "Mr. Wesley, did I see you give away the food for our day's journey? How shall we feed ourselves?"

"Well," the minister said, with a twinkle in his eye, "the season has produced a wonderful crop of blackberries. If the cottagers do not offer us hospitality, nature will."

A DANDY GETS AN ANSWER

In Somerset, not far from Bristol, the ancient town of Bath attracted dandies and ladies of London. Here it was that the Romans, long before, had built public baths over natural springs. Now the place was in a constant hubbub. There were sedan-chair bearers and mincing aristocrats. These went to gambling tables and dancing rooms. They fought duels with swords and pistols. Hairdressers strutted importantly from house to house during the mornings. They had to arrange enormous piles of hair, stuffed with ribbons, feathers and jewels, that sometimes made the ladies seven or eight feet tall. Wigmakers carried whitened curled wigs to the men. And dressmakers ran about with dolls dressed to show the latest styles to the women. Of the men who dictated the fashions of Bath, the finest "macaroni" of them all was Beau Nash.

But the work of the town had to be done, and the people who did it, as well as the farmers in the country nearby, were as poor

as lean street dogs. This was a time when farmers were hungrier than they had been a century before. Their common grazing lands had been taken from them by law and given to private owners. They could no longer find enough food for their cattle. And they still had to use wooden plows. Nowhere was the contrast between rich and poor, between idleness and drudgery, greater than in Bath.

John Wesley came to Bath to preach. In an open field, outside of town, he stood in the sunshine. A huge crowd of people, many ragged and unwashed but some neatly dressed, was waiting to hear him. It was an orderly crowd, though a little restless here and there. Word had gone about that Beau Nash would not permit a meeting of Methodists to be held.

Wesley began to preach, in his calm and powerful voice. The sound of French horns and horses' hoofs interrupted him. A procession of carriages and horsemen dashed into the crowd, scattering the people right and left. It drew up with a flourish in front of the little preacher. He stopped speaking and waited quietly as a man in a three-cornered white hat, dressed in satin and laces, stepped out of a carriage.

The man strode like a king to the front of the crowd, and asked arrogantly, "By what authority do you preach here?"

"By the authority of the Archbishop of Canterbury, who ordained me a minister of the Church of England," quietly replied the sober man in black.

"I say you are breaking the law. Besides, your preaching frightens people out of their wits."

"Did you ever hear me preach?"

"No," replied the dandy.

"How, then, can you judge of what you never heard?"

"Sir, by common report."

"Common report is not enough. Give me leave, sir, to ask — is your name Nash?"

"My name is Nash," the man said.

"Then, sir, I dare not judge *you* by common report."

Nash bit his lip as his friends standing near snickered behind their gloves. He turned on his heel furiously. "I desire to know what these people come here for?"

Before the preacher could reply, an old woman spoke up clearly, so that she could be heard far back in the crowd.

"Sir, leave him to me. You, Mr. Nash, take care of your body. We take care of our souls, and for the food of our souls we come here."

The crowd muttered approvingly, turning threatening eyes on the fine ladies and gentlemen who had come to witness the dismissal of the parson. Beau Nash strode to his carriage and flung himself inside without a word. John Wesley calmly took up his preaching where he had stopped. The sound of the carriages and horses died away. The crowd was quieted and listened to the little preacher with attention and great respect.

John Wesley's interest in children drew him to stay at a school whenever possible. Once Mr. Wesley visited a school kept by a friend, a Mr. Bush. As he was seated at tea in the parlor, two of the boys got into a fight in the yard. Mrs. Bush ran out and grasped them by the jackets, pulling them into the house. Mr. Wesley stood looking at them, teacup in hand. The boys grew quiet, heads ducked down, feet shuffling on the carpet.

Mr. Wesley went over to them and talked to them kindly. He asked them to be friends and to shake hands. The children clasped hands, but would not look at each other. Then John Wesley went to the table. He took a piece of buttered bread, folded it together, and asked the boys to share it.

"Now," he said, "you have broken bread together."

He gave them each a cup of tea, then put his hands on their heads and blessed them. The boys became friends. Next morning Mr. Wesley led the children in prayers. He called the two boys to him. He put his arms about their shoulders and gave them his blessing.

Everywhere there was much talk of this fearless minister. People seldom went to church, and when they did, they had to listen to long, dull sermons preached by indifferent ministers. These sermons meant nothing to those who heard them. But here was a man whose words seemed aimed at everyone present. He made them all believe that their lives had meaning to God and to themselves. More and more people came to hear him, even to dawn services. They came to the services conducted by Charles also.

John Wesley continued to travel. He went on long journeys, sometimes on foot, but usually on horseback. These journeys took him to all parts of England, Wales, Scotland, and Ireland. They made him the one man of that century who really knew the British Isles and its people.

Many English ministers were shocked by the new way of preaching, and wrote to John Wesley to tell him so. In answer to a letter from the Reverend James Hervey, in which he asked Wesley where his parish was, John Wesley wrote:

"I look upon all the world as my parish."

At about this time Samuel, the oldest Wesley brother, died. Samuel had never been sympathetic to the Methodist religious

movement. But John and Charles grieved for their brother. They also worried about their sisters, for the girls had all made unhappy marriages, except Anne and Kezia, who had died. But old Mrs. Wesley remained strong, and interested in her sons' work.

John's preaching took him away from London and his mother more than he liked. But he enjoyed his trips. They held good things and bad for him. One of the good things that meant much to him was the love given him by children. As John Wesley rode into a town his eyes brightened at sight of children running to greet him. He waved to them from his horse as they shouted, "Here comes our Mr. Wesley!"

And then he dismounted to stand among them and start singing. John and Charles had fine voices, and liked to sing. The hymns written by Charles and set to the music of popular tunes went out to village homes with the children. Their voices rose high and clear and crept into houses, drawing their elders into the streets and to meetings.

One old man asked the minister sourly, "Mr. Wesley, those rascals are like young demons. How can you get them singing like that?"

"To me they sound like angels in our Father's house," answered the minister with a smile.

The old man shrugged and grunted, "Sometimes they nearly push you over."

"In truth they do," John Wesley laughed. "Before preaching they only run around me and before me. But after preaching a whole troop of boys and girls will close me in, and will not be content until I shake the hands of each of them."

The man looked at Wesley in astonishment, as if thinking: What a strange thing! Everywhere the parson goes with his hymns, the children follow.

John Wesley told people: "Cleanliness is next to godliness." He said also: "Do all the good you can, in all the ways you can, in all the places you can, at all the times you can, to all the people you can, as long as ever you can."

Mr. Wesley had a custom of gathering children together in London to have tea with him. He had a great round teapot that, as one visitor said, "must hold a gallon." Before sitting down to tea and bread and butter, Wesley would join the children in singing a blessing:

> "Be present at our table, Lord,
> Be here and everywhere adored;
> These creatures bless and grant that we
> May feast in paradise with thee."

MOBS AND RIOTS

John Wesley decided to return for a few days to Epworth. He had not forgotten how his father had worked there, and how savagely the people had treated him. He asked his friend John Taylor to go with him.

But when they arrived in the village, the curate would not allow them to preach in the church. On the street John had been recognized and pointed out.

"There be John Wesley, son of our old parson! I would like right well to hear him preach," said a farmer to his wife.

That Sunday morning the church was crowded. The curate stiffly gave out a sermon in which he said that too much "enthusiasm" about preaching was a sin. There was a whispering passing through the church, for the people all knew that he meant the Wesleys. As people walked out into the noontime there stood John Taylor. He said quietly, "Mr. Wesley, not being permitted to preach in the church, expects to preach here at six o'clock."

At six o'clock people flocked into the churchyard. John Wesley was standing quietly on his father's large flat tombstone. A deep silence fell on the little churchyard.

John Wesley preached as he always did, simply and earnestly and with conviction. He did not shout and fling himself about and threaten with punishment from on high. He told the people that they, poor and unimportant as they were, were important to God. When he finished, as shadows fell across the peaceful spot, people came up to ask him to remain longer and to preach again.

He stayed seven days more. Every evening he preached on

his father's tomb. Then he went away with a feeling of happiness. For years both he and his father had preached and worked with these people, with no success. Now he could tell that they had not worked in vain.

As he jogged along the dusty road on his horse, with an open book in his hand, he said to himself: Now the fruit of our labors has appeared, and the seed sown so long ago has now sprung up.

When John returned to London he hastened to his mother, who was ill at their home in the Foundry. He was anxious to tell her of the experience in Epworth. But when he arrived he found her condition worse. She smiled, and her eyes brightened with pride as he told her of his preaching in Epworth. John was glad that she could hear of it now, for he could see that her life was nearly over. As John and Charles, with their sisters, sat beside their mother's bed, they all thought of the long years of loving service she had given to them. John thought also of the important part that she had played in the Methodist movement, and how much her advice and loyal help had meant to them.

Not long after his mother's death John Wesley went back to Newcastle, where he wanted to build a place of worship. He scarcely knew how it would be paid for, but he had the faith and courage to go ahead with the building of it. A Quaker who had heard of the plan sent Wesley a hundred pounds with a letter:

"Friend Wesley — I have had a dream concerning thee. I thought I saw thee surrounded with a large flock of sheep, which thou didst not know what to do with. My first thought when I awoke was, that it was thy flock at Newcastle, and that thou hadst no house of worship for them."

One of John Wesley's friends was Sophia Cooke. When she came to the Foundry in London, Wesley would greet her gaily with, "Live today, Sophy!" She had been a sad girl, seeing and feeling the troubles of all those around her. John Wesley was always cheerful and friendly. His advice to live well for each day brought a smile to her face and gave her courage. Sophy came from Gloucester. There she knew a man named Robert Raikes. He was as concerned with the bad conditions as she was.

One day, after Sophy returned to Gloucester, Robert Raikes looked with pity at the dirty, fighting children in the streets. He asked Sophy, "What shall we do for these poor neglected children?"

"Let us teach them to read, and take them to church."

So Robert Raikes started the first Sunday school in England. He lured the children to it by offering them buns and hot potatoes. Once there, he taught them to read and write, to do sums, and to learn the Scripture and to pray. After a short while the little school in Soot Lane was so large that "four decent women" were hired to conduct it.

John Wesley also felt that he must do something for children. His building in Newcastle was called the Orphan House. It stood just outside Pilgrim Gate, and it was here that Wesley established

82

a Sunday school in England. At that time many children were badly treated. Those of rich families were not thought to be important, and were kept out of sight as much as possible until they were grown up. But the children of the poor wandered the streets in vast hordes of ragged hungry waifs, thieving and fighting. Parents sold their boys for five pounds apiece, and girls for four, to be trained for chimney sweeps. At five years old children were often put to work down in the mines.

John Wesley also established the Kingswood School for boys, near Bristol. This was a boarding school where rules were strict, and life was not easy. Yet in this school there was no punishment by flogging, and no cruel treatment of the younger boys. Always there was justice and kindness. John Wesley had a study there, which he called his "sweet retreat."

Sunday schools were always important to John Wesley. He often talked to classes in them, in Bristol and in other towns. He called the Sunday schools his "nurseries for Christians."

The choir of the Orphan House at Newcastle became one of the best in the country. Miners and boatmen of the district were so eager to hear John Wesley preach that they would lie down on the benches after evening services and sleep there until the hour

83

for early morning service. During this time many Methodist Societies were organized through all that part of the country. Charles Wesley was traveling also, sometimes with his brother, sometimes alone, preaching and teaching his hymns to the people. He and John were making Methodism a singing religion.

But, for all this, things were not always easy for the Wesley brothers. Often mobs gathered, urged on by politicians who did not want people to be educated. John Wesley's forehead carried a scar, made by a stone flung at him. Once he was thrown into a horsepond. Charles Wesley said that he could tell the houses of Methodists by the marks of violence on them.

Sometimes preachers told crowds to stone the Methodists. These were the preachers who spent most of their time drinking, hunting, and gambling. Sometimes judges also persecuted Methodists. But there were others who did not approve of persecution.

Once John Wesley had a visit from a judge who said, "Sir, you have no need to suffer these riotous mobs to molest you, as they have done long. I and other magistrates have orders to do you justice whenever you apply to us."

Later the Methodists did apply for aid when ruffians tried to break up services, and some hoodlums were arrested.

Outside London crowds were sometimes violent. Wednesbury was a town where riots kept breaking out. John Wesley went there to help the Methodist Society. He preached once without trouble, but as he prayed afterward he heard the noise of a great mob, yelling and cursing. They shouted, "Bring out the parson. We will have that parson!"

John Wesley could look like a little fighting gamecock. He

walked quietly, but firmly and with flashing eyes, to the door. Flinging it open, he pulled a chair to it. He climbed upon the chair and stood there calling, "What do any of you want with me?"

The wild rough crowd was suddenly silent. This parson was so small, and yet he did not know fear! Some dropped their sticks and stones. But a man shouted, "You are breaking the law. Come to the judge with us, if you dare!"

Before John Wesley could speak, he heard a woman burst out, "This gentleman is an honest gentleman. We will spill our blood in his defense."

John Wesley stepped down. A crowd of people, suddenly friendly, surrounded him as he walked quietly toward the judge's house. The rest of the mob went home. It was dark, and torches swayed back and forth in the hands of the men, casting strange shadows on their wild faces.

At the judge's home a servant shouted from a window, "My master is abed. Go away!"

But the crowd wanted to prove the law, and see how the parson took it. They walked, with Wesley in their midst, to Walsall, a nearby village, to find another judge. Here a different mob appeared suddenly, and tried to take Wesley from the first one. The woman who had defended him leaped at the attackers and fought like a man. John Wesley stepped into a doorway and raised his voice. For a quarter of an hour he spoke to them, although at first he could not be heard in the uproar. The noise died down.

Unexpectedly a man cried out, "Sir, I will spend my life for you. Follow me, and not one soul here shall touch a hair of your head!"

86

They did not find a judge in Walsall who would come out, and so they started back for Wednesbury. But a Walsall mob followed them. As they tried to cross a bridge John Wesley looked down at the dark flowing river and wondered if he could swim across. But, because he was so short, many blows fell not on him but on others behind him. At last his new friends won the battle, and he was taken home.

As he saw the pale faces of his Methodist friends, who had thought him dead by now, he showed them his damages with a little smile. One flap of his waistcoat was gone, along with a little skin from his hand. He had had two hard blows on the head, but they had done no real damage.

"It is my rule," said John Wesley calmly, "always to look a mob in the face." He won many friends everywhere, in spite of riots and mobs, by his courage, and by his kindness.

Two days later in Wednesbury Charles asked the big man who had defended John, and who came then to join the Methodists, what he thought of John Wesley.

"What do I think of him?" boomed the man. "That he is a man of God. And God was on his side, when so many of us could not kill one man."

GOD'S GOOD RIDER

In some English villages a stone cross is placed in the square or green. This is called the market cross. Here, in the town of Bolton, in Lancashire, on the base of such a cross, John Wesley stood. It was a hot day, and the August sun beat down through dark green leaves of old trees. On the trampled grass a wild mob fought. They hooted and threw stones and tried to tear the little minister from his place on the base of the stone cross.

But there he stood, as firm as the cross itself. When three of the ruffians leaped up behind him they were the ones who received stones flung at John Wesley. One was shouting into the preacher's ear when a rock hit him on the cheek. A second was struck on the head just as he tried to push Wesley down. And a third received a blow on the hand as he reached out for the minister. All the while John Wesley preached on, calmly and confidently. After a time the people became quieter, and then began to listen to him.

Once, while preaching near Bedford, he was interrupted time after time. After a while he saw a rough man approach the front of the group. The man carried a small sack in one hand. Wesley saw him take from the sack some eggs and place them carefully in his pockets. Wesley went on preaching, but watched the man. He expected any minute to be pelted with eggs.

But there was a tall boy standing near the ruffian. He, too, had seen the eggs go into the pockets. Slowly he edged nearer and nearer. Then he gave a sudden jump, flinging his arms around the man in a tight bear hug.

"In an instant," chuckled Wesley later, as he told the story,

"the ruffian was perfumed all over, though it was not so sweet a perfume as balsam."

During many years John Wesley was called different things— "an enemy of the people," and others as bad. But he went on his way, paying no attention to them. His personal life was not happy. Charles had married a fine woman, and was living in Bristol. He did not travel so much now. But John had a wife who was so bad tempered that he could not live with her. His work was his whole life.

At a Methodist Conference John Wesley was asked this question: "What may we reasonably believe to be God's purpose in raising up the preachers called Methodists?"

Wesley pondered this for four days, praying, discussing it with his followers. Then he answered: "To reform the nation, more particularly the Church; to spread scriptural holiness over the land."

But there were those who did not want to see the nation

reformed. They did not like to have poor people think that they were as good as the upper classes. All sorts of disturbances were tried at his meetings. Bells were rung, ballad singers hired, mill-dams broken to flood the place of meeting, drums beaten. Yet nothing stopped the Methodists for long, and they usually came out of such contests the winner.

Once at a mine near Pembroke a dandified gentleman forced his way in and told the people roughly to go home and not to listen to these Methodists. At this the boy who drove the chaise, or carriage, in which John Wesley had come to the meeting, spoke up to reprove the man for his language.

The man snarled at him, "Do you think I need to be taught by a chaise boy?"

The boy looked him in the eye and answered calmly, "Really, sir, I do think so."

As the years passed, people became more friendly to the Methodists. After a time wild riots and street battles almost stopped. Methodism had spread from one end of the British Isles to the other. John Wesley continued to travel on an average of five thousand miles a year, preaching fifteen times a week or more. He had been ill twice, once when at Oxford, and again when he was fifty-one years old. Both times his illness had been tuberculosis. But he recovered from it completely. He felt that his early journeys, which accustomed him to cold and rain and wind, and preaching in the open, had toughened his body. They made it possible for him to endure hardships that most men could not have survived. And it was the outdoor life that kept him well.

John Wesley never owned much. He said with a smile, "I get all I can, and give all I can; that is, all I have."

Until he was seventy years old, Wesley journeyed on horseback, book in hand. There were no roads passable enough for a carriage in the north of England, and the coach went only as far as York.

Wesley always rose at four in the morning, and seldom went to bed before midnight. Sometimes he had accidents, when his horse went lame, or suddenly fell upon its head, as at Bristol once.

But Wesley got up unhurt and preached to seven thousand people.

John Wesley always considered the Methodist Societies as part of the Church of England. When the American colonies began their fight for independence, Wesley was not in sympathy with it. He advised the Methodists to support the king. After the Revolution was over, however, he accepted the new country, and helped establish the Methodist Church in America as a separate church.

As the minister grew old, roads all over England were improved, and he traveled more often by carriage. He fitted out one end of his carriage with a writing table and bookshelves. Once, when he was eighty-three years of age, he was in a carriage on his way to preach at St. Ives. The storms had been so severe that the lowlands were flooded and the driver feared to attempt the trip. An hostler at the London Inn offered to drive the minister. But when they reached Hayle they found that the low, sandy area was covered with the tide, and the driver feared that they could not cross to St. Ives. The old man thrust his head from the window. With the salty wind blowing his long white hair, he called, "Take the sea, take the sea!"

"Sir," shouted the driver, "the horses must swim, then, for the waters are very deep, and rising."

"What is your name, driver?" asked the minister.

"Peter, sir."

"Then, Peter," called the old man in a firm voice, "fear not, thou shalt not sink."

The driver whipped up his horses and they swam across. The water came into the carriage, and the driver held his breath for

92

fear that they would be drowned. But the storm died down, and they reached the other side safely. When they arrived at the inn, John Wesley saw to it that the driver and his horses were fed and warmed before he took care of his own needs. Then he went to the chapel to preach.

In these later years Wesley's visits to far parts of England were occasions for general rejoicing in the communities that he visited. The mobs had disappeared. He was the best beloved man in all England. This pleased him, and he enjoyed greeting his friends again.

The slave trade, in which hardened sea captains captured African natives and sold them, John Wesley called, "that execrable sum of all villainies." With letters, pamphlets, and his writings for the Society for the Suppression of the Slave Trade, he fought a constant war against slavery as an institution.

In all his travels John Wesley kept writing in his journals. They told not only of what he did and thought, but of the life of the people he met day by day. These journals, at the time of his death, numbered twenty-six bound volumes.

John Wesley lived during most of the eighteenth century. During this time hardy English traders had sailed to undiscovered lands. The American colonies had become the United States. The French Revolution had taken place. John Wesley had seen the coming of the steam engine, and inventions of machines for making cloth. He had been interested from the first in Benjamin Franklin and his experiments in electricity. He had watched England change as people went to work in factories. He saw canals and roads open up wild country. He lived when great artists and writers

were picturing England. Yet it was John Wesley, and his brother Charles, who made people aware of their responsibilities to God and to their fellow men. And it was these two who gave people a singing religion.

For many years John and Charles Wesley shared their work and their thoughts. When John was eighty-five years old, Charles was taken seriously ill. John was away in Shropshire preaching when his brother died. Although Charles had not accompanied him on his travels for some time, John missed his brother sadly. But he knew that Charles was with him in spirit.

John was especially fond of his niece Sarah, the daughter of Charles. She was growing up to be a fine, intelligent girl. She sometimes traveled with her uncle, and he discussed with her his hopes for public education. She read books with him, and helped him put the books into simple language for the people. John Wesley published more than four hundred books for the people, and also edited a magazine. The money from the publications was used to aid church work.

Among the books that were most interesting to Sarah, as well as to John Wesley, were those on medical subjects. Wesley was the first to open a dispensary where poor people could get medicines free of charge.

John Wesley continued to preach and to travel almost until his death. He preached his last sermon when he was eighty-eight years old, only a week before he died. That same week he wrote his last letter in which he urged a fight on the slave trade.

And then for several days he felt weak and ill. Once he roused to sing a hymn. And then he said, "The best of all is, God is with us."

On the second day of March, 1791, the old minister wakened to see several of his friends and relatives standing by his bed.

John Bradford said softly: "Lift up your heads, O ye gates; and be ye lift up, ye everlasting doors; and this heir of glory shall come in." As he spoke, John Wesley said again, "The best of all is, God is with us." Then he closed his eyes and seemed to sleep.

John Wesley had said that he wished no crowd at his funeral. So his friends buried him at night in the yard of the City Road Chapel, just across the street from the grave of his mother. In England, in Scotland, in Ireland, and across the seas in America, people mourned his passing.

On a tablet placed in honor of John and Charles Wesley in famous Westminster Abbey, in London, are John Wesley's words:

"I look upon all the world as my parish."